Stuck in the World
All Alone

By
Alrick Hollingsworth

A Young Urban Author Publication

Copyright 2012

Alrick Hollingsworth

Cover Design: Fusion Creative Works

Developmental Editor: Dr. Jeffrey Perkins Jr.

Publisher: Young Urban Authors

www.youngurbanauthors.org

ISBN-13:978-1481205986

ISBN-10:1481205986

Library of Congress Control Number (applied for)

CONTENTS

Dedication

I dedicate this book to my great grandma Christine and my grandma Johnnie. They were the strongest and most beautiful women that I'll know in this life time. I will always love them and keep them in my heart.

I also would like to thank this special person who really put effort in my life and would help my family tramindously and her name is cindy varter and I love her for all her support. thank you cindy thank you very much.

Acknowledgements

I would like to acknowledge a couple of people in my life. I would like to start off with my dad because he was there for me, my whole life, and some kids don't have their parents. I love that my mom has been clean and sober for six years on December 13. I love her for that. I love all my aunts and uncles but I have one uncle that is the coolest uncle in the world, when he is not drinking. When he is drunk he turns into a whole different person and starts reminiscing on my grandma and his sister Cassandra and start talking about "sandy bandy I love you my sister " "Momma I love you. So basically if you are my family I wrote this for you. But I love my grandma Johnnie for all that she did for me and I just am thankful just to be a grandson of a woman so strong.

Introduction

This book is based on a true life story and is about a young man who lives in Seattle, Washington all of his life. He goes through a lot of trials and tribulations with his family and within his own life. He has a mom that is on all kinds of different drugs and she goes to jail for 2 years and then his dad has another baby with this girl he found. Then my mom leaves him because of the girl's background. His mom finds the strength and stays clean and sober. He loses his auntie Cassandra. 4 years after that his grandmother dies from cancer and the family goes through a whole bunch of blaming people on how it happened and the family gets disconnected like leaves on a tree in the middle of fall. While he is transitioning back and forth between his mom and dads house he has to try to keep sane and hope that the family will become a close knit family again.

OPENING POEM

I'm stuck in this world all alone

I'm a young man in the body but in mind I'm grown.

I'm nothing to play with

Like a broken collar bone

It's ringing all you got to do is pick up the phone

Girls is young messin with dudes that are grown.

I'm in my own zone

I'm enjoying my young life

and like Peter Pan I'm not trying to be grown.

When my grandma died I felt all alone.

My name is Alrick and I'm stuck in this world all alone

Trying to make it up to heaven hoping God don't judge me wrong

PART ONE: ALL ALONE

Hi, my name is Alrick Hollingsworth and this short story that you're about to read is about me; a portrait of my life as seen through the eyes of my youth.

For instance, my favorite color is dark red and I've enjoyed its color all my life. My favorite food is my mom's cooking and I especially like her corn bread ~~and~~ Cause when you bite into it, it melts on your tongue just like hot butter. I am a dancer, writer, and I'm pretty fit for my age. Even though I'm good at sports, it's hard to believe that I'm scared of heights for some reason. Moreover, I like Hip Hop, Rhythm and Blues (little soul music), but I mostly I like all music!

I remember the first time I got a dog. It was a girl...a red nose "pit-bull" with blond hair and belly white fur. I lived on 24th and Pike and remember it today like it was yesterday. My dad had a Cadillac Brougham with 100 gold spoke hub caps; but not just any gold 100 spokes, they were four times gold plated and the car was all white with burgundy pin stripes, on each side, and a burgundy soft top. My dad was a big time dope dealer and owned a store. I was the only child at the time and even though I was a spoiled brat, I still had respect for my elders, and I still do today.

Back in 2000, I was just a child living in a pink colored cement apartment. It was me, my mom, my pit-bull Red and I really did love Red!

My dad had the apartment up stairs and my Great Grandma Chris she lived in the apartment down the hall across from us. There was a white kid who lived next door to my grandmother and me. We used to play with each other; and even though he was older than me, since I liked playing with older people, I thought nothing of it.

Then the white people moved away from that apartment. My dad was a business owner and off-side dope dealer. And since I was the only child, I was also a spoiled brat who got everything I wanted. For instance, I wanted and I got a Benz on my birthday that was powered by charging the battery. Then, my cousin...Man-Man...he broke it!

Out of all my cousins...Donny (D-Mula)...Taush...and Shantia (Tia), Man-Man was Grandma Chris's favorite...but she loved us all. My dad is Alrick Hollingsworth (Rick-Rock), and my mom is Christal Fields (C-money). How my mom and dad met up is a cold story.

It started when my mom was supposed to help one of her friends come in and rob my dad blind but

because my dad had so much game, my mom said she didn't want to do it even though I guess her friends still went on and robbed him. Nevertheless,

17

my mom and dad decided to stay together. But all this happened before I was born and I'm just now getting bits and pieces of the story.

However, in 2000, my mom was a dope-fiend. She was also a cold hustler and that's why my dad messed with her because he was a cold hustler too. But when you put both of them together; well, that's a different story.

As children, we would roll through the town on roller skates we kept in my dad's car. But he soon lost it when he and Grandma Johnnie went to Muckleshoot and sold it. That's also when my dad started having gambling problems, and we soon moved to and from places and my dad moved to State street, in a

duplex and my mom lived right down the street in a one bed room shack. That's when she enrolled me in John Muir elementary school. Shortly afterwards I remember being in an after school homework club when one day a white boy slapped me he in my face hard like I was a grown man even though I was only five years old. He was much older and had to be at least twelve years old. When my mom came in the classroom she did not know that I'd just been slapped and I wasn't going to tell her because she was using drugs.

Although I hated it when she gave that boy a Krispy kreme donut, she then gave me a donut and a toy robot, and that worked, for calming me down. Krispy kreme donuts were my most favorite things to eat besides my grandmother Johnnie's cooking. But when my mom looked at me and said "what's wrong with your face!" I replied, "the white boy slapped me," and she flipped out!

She asked him "what if I slapped you in your punk ass face? Why did you even hit my baby in the face? For real how old is your big ass?" And then she started talking about getting my big brother...but she gave

19

my brother up for adoption at birth because she was on drugs, and the same thing happened with my sister. But she was lucky to have my grandmother...my grandmother Mary Fields who

took my sister in custody and raised her to be the woman that she is today. But this was

a drop ass adoption this was like go away because boy

But I was put in the same position as the rest of them and I was glad and so thankful for my dad being a man and stepping up to the plate to take care of me. He stopped all his bad habits to take care of me and my sister. But that's longer down the line. Yet from

Baby sister kiki

that point on I was loved by my dad and my Grandma Johnnie because my mom had started going in and out of doing drugs and arguing with my dad.

At this time my dad still had the store and his jerry curl but he was losing hair because he was stressing

20

at the time about my mom and her drug use. From that point, there was no more seeing my mom unless it was on the 'Mad block' back when Deano's was open and the corner store with an Asian man and a fat cashier. I remember one time going down to the 'mad block' looking for my mom. She was at this boarded up house sitting on the stairs with one roller blade on one foot, and the other foot was swollen possibly from shooting so much dope!

I said to her, "Hi mom...why do you have only one shoe on?" She replied. "I hurt my foot baby and now I can't walk...so I just roll around on this one foot."

So I said to her. "No you don't mom, get on my back and I'll take you where you want to go." At the time of all this, I was seven years old and my mom must have weighed 80 pounds. So she got on my back and I walked her to the corner store and then stopped to put her down to tell her to go to the hospital to get her foot fixed. But I know she didn't go. So I went to the 'mad block' with my dad and walked around with him, we got by Deano's and my dad decides to go to Ed's mom's house and kick it with him.

Ed had this pit bull that was named Danger. The dog had a big head and an all white stomach with a blond back. He was big and buff with all muscles and a big jaw. I think the dog pound put him to sleep because he bit someone. My dog was the best dog ever but my dad used to beat up the dog every time it did something wrong. But after a while we moved up to State Street and so did my mom but she lived in the house down the street in the shack...that's what we used to call it, while my dad lived down the street from my mom in a duplex house. At age five to go to school, I'd walk up the street to catch the bus. I was going to John Muir elementary. But one day I missed

[handwritten margin note: I loved that dog but only a while it want crazy because he was sold]

[handwritten note above "shack": snack]

22

the bus and was crying on my way back home because I thought I was in trouble.

The neighbor up the street near my bus stop saw me crying and gave me a ride to school. Then I was okay until I got to school and had to go use the bathroom. While in the bathroom, I used it on myself, and it even gets worst when I went to the office because all they had where panties so I had to wear pissy panties until I got home. My dad must have told everybody in Seattle about what happened to me. So I went home to my moms and she told me to take a bath and put on some boxers.

When I got out the tub my mom had a present for me, a DVD player and I was happy because I had a collection of Scooby Doo movies. I guess my mom had bought it from someone. So I put a movie in and a roach started crawling out of the DVD player then I looked and it had a whole nest of them on the inside,

23

and we threw it away in the trash because my mom freaked out. She hates bugs.

We didn't have any bugs at my mom's house until that DVD player popped up. We took the Scooby Doo movie out first because I loved me some Scooby Doo. But at my dad's house one day there was a whole bunch of bugs in the refrigerator because the

power was cut off. They were ants! Because my dad had hustled to get the bill paid, one thing I can say is that my dad always will take care of his kids no matter what. I remember when my mom and dad got into a fight over something and my dad went out

side and threw a dirt ball on his chess and called the police. Because she had got my dad arrested before, when they came my dad said she threw a dirt rock at him and they put my mom in hand cuffs. But my dad told them not to take her to jail and they didn't. After that, my mom never called the police on my dad again. One day my auntie green eyes came over to my mom's house and I guess they were close friends and she had stolen something from her boy friend and while I was in the bathroom she was getting beat up by him. All the while I was locked in the bathroom, all I could here was "my son is here ya'll gotta get out of here with this shit...oh hell no put that gun away for I call the police...my baby is in the bathroom!"

Also one night I remember my dad and mom got in to a fight and he went home and came back around 11:00 at night. There were a whole bunch of *smokers*.....

in my mom's house, and when my dad came back the swat team came straight through the door waiving AK-47s with lasers on the end and waiving pistols. They wore all black. Took all the grown-ups and searched every one and ordered us all to sit on ten chairs. One of the police said to my dad..."remember me." And after that, my mom went to jail. I didn't see her for a while and that's when my dad and this girl named Kenyata got together.

Kenyata was no average person. She was a crack head and a cold piece of work. She would do anything for anybody and she was nasty. She wouldn't clean up or nothing. She was like night and day when compared to my mom. I don't know how my dad got her pregnant, and I truly believe it was out of loneliness for my mom and it was an accident.

When my mom was in jail my dad moved all her stuff in his house, because all the crack heads were trying

to take over her house. While she was in jail for about a month or so, I visited her to see if she was okay. In a visit my mom asked me "should I go into treatment?" And I said "yes." But while she was in jail, my dad got Kenyata pregnant with my little sister Kiki.

Kenyata was the only girl my dad had arguments with because she would wait until my dad went to sleep and take his crack sack, go smoke it up, and come back when it's gone. Even though my dad would whoop her ass, that didn't help much because she'd just kept doing it. She would only get beat up either when she would smoke crack while pregnant with my little sister or turn dates and not come back home for days at a time and all smoked out. *return*

Then when she had the baby my dad took my sister and he raised her. ~~Her mom stopped coming to see her and then my mom got out and didn't want to be~~ with my dad any more. *Then my dad & she they asked for her so change kiki's diaper and she went to the bathroom window and jumped out the window then I didn't see her for 5 years.*

My dad always said that it was because of me telling lies on him, all the time, that that's why they would get into arguments. But it was really because of Kenya~~gh~~ta.

27

When my mom saw her she said "hell no," and she did not mess with him anymore. But my mom was cool enough to take care of my baby sister even though everyone said she was stupid. My mom would always say "it is not the baby's fault she is here now. Then my dad moved to the Crescents and

my mom moved to a clean and sober house on Langston Road; my grandmother Johnnie went on to live in Skyway. This is when my mom started messing with a guy named Darryl that everybody called *Double Barrow* because he was a hell-of-a-bluff for no telling reason.

In the Crescents' apartments, the most ghetto place I'd ever seen in my life, it was a cold place to stay. There was a dope crack house on the second floor and a weed house. The second floor also had another crack house at the end of the hallway.

28

There were always fights and gun shots heard around the place. ~~Even though they had police in~~ *Police housed* their *and* all the smokers that lived their whenever the police come in they didn't go to jail. Most of the smokers were already snitches and we had hoe's living right next to us, in which the mom and daughter would get in to fights. Some hoe's living next to me one day gave me a ~~fireworks~~ *Blackcut* and told me to throw it but it blew up in my hand.

Then I got into a fight with this one guy and when he brought out a knife, I ran in the house and stayed inside. The next day we were cool and started kicking it again. There was a fence next to the

apartment and on the other side ~~was~~ of it was a house with bushes all around it. We would kick a hole in the fence and sneak into *the* a house on the other side. One time I found a gun there but I left it alone and left. When I came back it was gone; although I think one of *my homey's* got it. The next time we went in the house it looked like a person was living there and that's when I stopped going in the house with them.

I had an auntie that lived up the street, I called her Auntie Shaunie. She had, I don't know how many kids but I knew Dayton, Savion, Nelly Blue, Kameo Lil Nut, and Jaylen. Every time my dad would go to the casino and not be at the house after school, I would go up to my aunties house and kick it with my cousins. I had some fun times at my Auntie Shaunie's

house and that's where I learned how to fight.

Also, almost every time it snowed my cousins and I would get together and go sliding down this big hill and have snow ball fights. Across the street there was a store that was named Bobs market and the lady that owned it was named Mamma. She was so nice to me. Every time I came over she would say "hi baby," and the days when my dad was broke I could get stuff from her to eat. She was cool.

Dareold's

~~Darryl's~~ brother stayed right behind the corner store. His brother's name was Donald and his son little Donald and I used to go over to their house and kick it with little Brian. At Big Brian's house they used to cook some good food all the time, especially BBQ. Plus they had a big trampoline in front of their house with a huge pit-bull. Big Brain was a good boxer as far as I know, and Little Brain was a good boxer himself. Little Brian was ~~fourteen~~ same age as me.

Sixteen

One time I got into a boxing match in front of CT's house and I just kept socking his gut and he was tagging my face in. So, we stopped. I remember the first time I put on the gloves with Shaunie's son Savion. He busted my lip but it was okay. However, Dazion and I got into many fights. I would win some time because I would over power him to the point of taking him to the ground. He would win because

31

he'd wait until I got tired. That's when he'd start giving me shots until I dropped down, and then he'd stop. But I cool. I just checked my face and was ready for another round.

When I left John Muir, I went to Emerson. I remember a talent show they had, and I chose to rap and even though my cousin battled me, I still think that I won. By the way, that was in the 5th grade. I graduated and went to Aki for my first year of middle school. On my first day, there were these boys on the

bus and they asked me "Do you smoke weed?" In which, I said "yea...sometimes"....That's when they said to me "no you don't." And ever since then, *my homey* and I smoked every day before school. We got on the school bus "keyed", then up and went to class high as hell! I never got caught until one time when he gave me some weed to hold for him until after school so we can smoke. I remember going to

32

the bathroom to put it in a container so it wouldn't stink, but it all spilled in my back pack. Because I was already high, when I got to class I was still high and smelled like weed. The administrators pulled me out of class and started talking to me saying "woooo...woo...you smell like straight up weed...and you look high. Why you can't even stand up straight...come on let's call your parents and you're getting suspended." That's when they searched me. But because I had the weed in my pants they did not find it.

Another time I got caught was when I put some kool

aid in some codeine bottles and called it some syrup. I pulled it out in art class and then the same boy from the bus asks for some. He drank it while it was in my bag and the art teacher got wind that something's up and he called the administrator to come and search my bag. The administrator found the syrup bottles and I got long term suspension for bringing drugs like that to school, even though it was just a bottle of codeine with Koolaid in it, I got in serious trouble.

One time while I was in class, this boy was throwing stuff at me. I pulled out a cap gun and pointed it at him and put it back in my bag. Then he threw something again but the teacher saw him and she said "get out of my class." And he replied "well...he pulled out a gun and pointed it at me"...and

adding..."it's in his back pack!" So again the teacher called the administrator and they came and took me to the office.

They tried searching me and told me to take off my coat. I remember telling them, "my dad said I don't have to take off any of my clothes for anybody." And that's when he grabbed my coat, unzipped it, and slammed me to sit in a chair. Then I was told to call my mom and dad and tell them "to come down here because they want to talk to you."

They searched me without my parents in the room and they were not supposed to do that. Next they put me in the retard class until my mom got there and then they got a metal detector and scanned me. I was so glad that cap guns are made of plastic. They didn't detect anything; so I was good, because I had hidden it in my waist pants all the while.

After that I went to the 7th grade. One day everybody was in the lunch rooms and this one boy was spreading the word "the dogs are coming to sniff out the school for drugs," and stuff like that, and that's when me and this other boy left to go hide our weed. I remember walking in the hall across from the lunch room and him throwing his in the garbage. But I guess while we were in class they found it. Next, they must have had someone with a phone stake out the garbage can to see who went there to find the weed.

So during the next period, when I went to see if the weed was still there, I see the fool that was supposed to set me up, and I just let it alone and kept walking to class. But right after class, I went there and just

pulled the whole bag out of the trash and threw it on the ground. However, while walking to the front of the school, as I was leaving a police officer pulls me into the office. He wanted to talk about what happened, how it happened, and I again was suspended for it. Thus, my middle school year was just a whole bunch of mischief and filled with not doing the right stuff.

Then from the house on Langston Street my mom moved in with her boyfriend Darryl. He was working at the Grayline Station and was he getting paid. I remember one day, the first time I drove a car was with Darryl and my mom. We drove up to a school but a couple weeks after that Darryl had got high and started smoking crack and locked us out the house.

36

We couldn't get back in because my mom was not on the lease and that was the coldest feeling in the world. I couldn't believe that he had the locks

changed, while we were sleep at a neighbor's house.

I remember saying to her "give me the key mom," and I tried it and that's when I figured that that dude had changed the locks on my mom with all her stuff inside. Wow! That's when my mom moved to Tukwila into a big four bedroom house with one

of her co-workers named Anna.

However, I also remember having had some good times there. I used to go down the street to play with *my homey* Zack and he had everything a kid could want. He had guns, a trampoline, all the games an Xbox 360, Ps3, and the wii. But we never stayed in the house too often. We either were riding the four wheeler or the dirt bikes. Sometimes we would have bee-bee gun fights. My

mom's roommate Anna and her really did become best friends. After a while everything was cool in the house and my mom left Darryl eold and got with this dude named Michael.

My dad didn't like Michael at all for some reason and came to find out that he was a cheater. Even though my mom stayed with him for three years, she got hurt over and over by him until she caught him with some girl she seen him with and finally left Michael. Anna started bringing this man over that she liked but they were not supposed to be together because they work together. So they would sneak and see each other at night and go out for dinner and stuff like that. Little did Anna knew that the man she was messing around with was a married man and she ended up pregnant and had a miscarriage. But they still stayed together for a long time and she ended up having another child by the guy. It didn't take Anna that long for the guy's wife to get the news and Anna still stayed with him even though she knows it was a double negative with her job and with God's business when you get married. I guess they were that much in love. Even when they were stressing about dealing with the wife, me and Michael was painting the room and getting it ready for the baby.

And when Anna was having the baby her mom came from Portland to see it be delivered, and so did my mom and the baby's dad. Everything seemed cool until Anna moved out of town to live with her mom. Even though the baby's dad sends her money he neglects the baby. Every time Anna wanted to talk to him he didn't answer the phone and he told her to quit texting him. He later changed after she left town. So whenever Anna's back in town she calls the wife to let her know that she has been messing around with him and that they have been doing it for a long time. She also mentioned that they have a baby together. After the wife heard that, she relapsed, again started smoking crack. Now that everything is in the air he still sends money but avoids Anna and the baby.

My mom and Michael seemed to be a good couple they had fun with each other and spend a lot of time with each other. But every time my mom put some good looking clothes on he would say that she looked whorish and start tripping because he wanted her to take them off. I wondered at times if it was because he was the one cheating on my mom.

My mom's reaction to him would be that she doesn't like that type of stuff he wanted her to wear, and then more weird sh*t would start happening. For instance, we'd get in his car and he didn't want anyone to touch the windows. He treated his car better than he treated my mom and that's another thing she didn't like about him. We also noticed that every time my sister Destiny and me came over he would act funny, like he wanted all the attention from my mom himself, and when all of us went to the store he always hurried us up to leave.

Once my mom said she wanted him to move in with her because of Anna's leaving and the bills were so high. However, he told her "no" because he had his own apartment downtown. So my mom said, "That's some weird sh*t." And that's when she started

suspecting something was going on. She started asking her friends about him and some people were saying he was gay. So she told my dad to ask some men about him to see if he was or not and my dad said the people he asked said yes he is. That's when my mom is thinking this *dude is* gay and sh*t like that.

Next, she started checking his phone numbers but every time she touched it they would get into an argument with her about touching his phone. Then she started saying he was cheating so one night she had called him and he didn't answer his phone. Since she thought he was sleeping, she didn't think anything of it. However, because her job is right by his house she stopped when she'd seen someone outside in his truck.

That's when she decided to circle the block and when she came back around she saw it was him in his truck with another female. From her car she flashes while saying "you're nasty ," I knew your butt was cheating!" And that's when she left him. But she also gave him another chance. It happened like this. One day while he was at the 1504 Club, he forgot his phone was on the counter. While he was shooting pool, a girl texted him and my mom saw it. That's when she started *flashing* in the 1504 Club; put his business on blast, and left him for good.

But also at this time, my auntie Cassandra was in the hospital and in bad condition. She was not scared to die and she stayed strong until the end. We used to go visit her and ride on the back of her wheel chair. She would take us to the vending machine and buy us whatever we wanted. She was so strong then, within a month or two later she passed away. My Auntie Cassandra ~~was~~ will be dearly missed.

But before she fell ill and went to the hospital, she was a cool person that you never messed with. She did not care what anybody thought about her. If she wanted to wear one side of her ~~hair cut~~ head and the other side pressed with white ~~face~~ paint on ~~it~~ her face that is what she would wear. At the funeral she looked so beautiful and looked like she was at rest. She was my favorite auntie. She was real mellow and even

43

though other people called her crazy, I loved her cause she was strong at least in my eye sight.

I lost a lot of women in my family. My Grandmother Johnnie was the next best woman next to my mother.

She kept it real and she was the only one who could get me out of one of my dad's real butt whooping. I have a Great Grandma Chris whom I also loved dearly. She taught us to keep it in the family, and she had the best cookouts in the world! I really loved how she would cook for all the holidays; I mean huge dinners that were so much food we would even feed the neighbors.

I also have a living grandmother Mary, although she meanest to me has been the farthest from me. She is my mom's mother, but things in the past with my mom's drug use have somehow separated us. I tried to bond with Grandma Mary many times. I see her

44

sometimes, but she makes it hard and I feel sad that I
have a grandma living that I don't even know.

I finally gave up, it was much too hard. Although I
remember when I was about five years old calling
her a name on the phone because she would not let
me speak to my big sister Destiny. Every since then
she would leave me in a corner on time out and that
was nine years ago. I hope before she dies that I will
be able to be a grandson to her, if she lets me.

Grandma Mary really makes me feel like I am in this
world all alone. I have had three grandmas and she's

the only one that has pushed me away and it hurts
me, my mom, and my sister too. I thank God that I
got my Auntie Shaunte that is also my moms only
sister. She is the only one I stay in close touch with
on my mom's side and she has a son named
Armonte. Oh, my mom's cousin Niecey she also
comes around from time to time with her kids. I am

so proud of my mom cause after she went to treatment at Drug Court the last time, she has been clean and sober every since. It will be five years and eight months now. God works in mysterious ways cause my mom got back with Darryl after three years and I believe now she's happy again. I can't believe that it happened...and not that it's bad. I just never thought that she would ever go back to him; she never gave my dad another chance and he still loves her.

PART TWO: TURNED OUT

I was about eleven when I started becoming a weed head. My mom and dad did not know that I smoked because I used to go over to my cousins house where we would smoke together. I remember one time I got caught and here's what happened. I went over to my cousin's house and we were kicking it with his girlfriend at her dad's house.

I remember leaving them alone and went to the park and seen some people dancing but they were older and had better dancing skills than me. So I tried to battle them anyway in order to learn some new moves and get experience. We battled for about thirty minutes. Then Man-Man called and I left to go back over to his girlfriend's house. Once there, we all went upstairs to watch TV, while he rolled up a *blunt*. We smoked it and his girlfriend broke out the liquor her dad had. We all took a drink and that was my first time drinking.

So while I was over at his girl's house, high and drunk as hell, my dad calls and says that I have to come to my grandmother's house and he's going to pick me up. I must have tried everything to get the liquor smell off my breath so I wouldn't get my butt

whooped! I used toothpaste and mouthwash and I ate something to try to get the smell out. So by the time I left and started walking to my grandmother's house, which was right up the street, my dad was already there by the time I got there.

As I walked into the house he was sitting at the table with grandma and he was smoking a *blunt* himself! I walked by him and he said, "turn you're a*s back around and come here," and that's when

he smelled my breath to see if I had been drinking.

Sure enough he smelled not only the liquor but the

weed as well. Now, I was in double trouble! But

this is one reason that I loved my Grandma

Johnnie, because no matter what I did, and how

bad it was, she would just say "Ricky...don't do

it...Ricky...." I could hear her in my head like a Broken

~~stadium crowd cheering on a winning team~~...I Record that want to keep playing

really do miss her so much.

 I didn't see Man-Man for hell-of-a while after that,

and I didn't get the butt whooping of my life.

Although that was weird and I was nervous

because my dad was the type that lets all kind of

stuff build up inside, so when you got whooped

you got hammered!

The same house that my grandmother lived in my

dad

49

was outside one night and the Mexican people who lived next door had got into disagreement over something and started fighting right in the middle of the street. One of them stabbed the other one and then they stopped for a minute. The one that got stabbed was saying something to the other person and then the ambulance came and took him to the hospital; and after that, the people living there ~~they~~ moved.

But the day before they left the girls that lived there came over and invited me over to the house. There was not that much in it and I guessed that they already started moving. When we went into the garage, I saw a hell-of-a fire extinguisher and tools. After that they took me back and I still don't know why they came and got me and my cousin Tinka. Tinka used to go down to Skyway park and kick it. She had a friend that lived near there, so when we went to play with her and have fun at

the park, most of the time we would go by

ourselves and just kick it. I remember when I first

start playing football for the Renton Rangers. Even

though I sucked at it I still played.

One day after practice this boy was like the best

dancer on the team. So we battled. But when I

was battling I had lost track of time and forgot that

I need to be at my grandma's right after practice.

So my dad came down to the park to find me and

he said, "if you don't get your tale up to your

grandma's house right now I'm gonna beat you're

a*s!" And I ran to get my shoulder pads and

helmet and continuing running all the way to

grandmas. Once again grandma had saved me and

said, "don't whoop him Ricky...". Tinka and me are

best cousins for life no matter who or what comes

between us. One time we were having so much fun that we laughed the whole car ride. When my little sister got in the car, we suddenly stopped and started up again. I think we were high from all that weed my grandma was smoking. We were best cousins and we did all kind's of stuff. Like one day for instance we were supposed to go to the store and get some popcorn and something to drink so we can all watch a movie.

But while we were walking down the street I was lighting up pieces of pepper and throwing the matches on the ground. While we were walking by these sticker bushes, I lit a match and threw it in a bush. The whole side of that fence caught fire and

Tinka and me both tried to put it out. I ended up running to the store and bought a water bottle to pour it on the fire and put it out. But that didn't work.

52

Next, we tried throwing dirt on it. That too didn't work. But a lady across the street saw us and called the fire truck to come and put out the fire. I remember us running back to my Grandma Johnnie's house and we told my cousin Tia that someone else started a fire. When she got us to finally tell the truth, she went and told grandma and my dad. But again, my grandma said, "don't whoop him Ricky."

However, I do remember one time when we lived on Pike Street her and my cousin Darnell made me and Tinka eat ants, and the next day I got chicken pocks and had to go to the doctor. They told me

what it was and that it will go away soon and it will be my last time that I will get the chicken pocks. I never told on her about that. So ever since my grandma moved to a house over by this day care, we used to have some parties and just straight up crack up but in a old school way. I remember my auntie Lanice came in a fishnet outfit without any bra on or panties. So everything was out there. But even though my grandma was watching us and paying attention to everybody, she got all her kids

together to play *tonk*, it was like when we were very young kids, everybody in the house played cards and gambled. Although when someone got broke, my grandma would let them borrow money so they can get back in the game and everything was cool.

Afterwards, everyone started leaving at the same time and mom was saying you don't have to go so nobody thought anything of it. But my grandma was trying to spend time with us while she can but we had school and my dad had to go meet somebody.

I used to ride in the car no matter what time it was. I would wake up and get in the car and ride with dad to go get my grandma's and smoke a blunt. That was my grandma's favorite medicine and she loved Crown Royal and used to go to the wormhole to get what she wanted. My sister, dad, and I used to take grandma to Virginia Mason to go for her chemo therapy. Only my sister and I didn't know how serious it was.

We used to be on floor playing around and making all kinds of noise. When the chemo therapy

person said that the cancer had gone away, my grandma was getting stressed out and her nerves had gotten bad. But this time when she went to get a check up the doctor said that she had cancer ~~came back~~. ~~again~~. ~~This~~ Time it was way to severe and she didn't have much time to live.

55

My grandma was a strong woman and she didn't let cancer hold her back from anything. She even went and voted for Obama for President as sick as she was. She also was still trying to pay the bills, the car note, and start an insurance policy so that we do not have to pay anything for her grave or anything else. However, my grandma was getting sicker and sicker. The cancer was eating her up from the inside and there was nothing that we could do about it but show her how much we loved her.

Christmas came and my grandma was in her bed and could not go and get us presents. So she sent my auntie to the store to go and get them. My auntie went and got the presents and gave them to us from mom.

My grandma was a rider, and she was holding on to life as long as she could just to make sure that we where okay before she passed. When she was on her death bed, she was still trying to give the little game that she had left before it was too late, but it already was. I remember her asking my dad, "what are you and your brother gonna do with these women that you

have?" And she also asked, "why don't we celebrate my Auntie Cassandra's birthday?" when she died ~~because we~~ _when we_ didn't while she was alive. My dad could not answer. My dad's woman is a

strawberry at least that's what my dad called her. My dad had the most messed up relationships that I've ever seen in my life.

Kenyata would sit around the house and not take a bath or nothing. Every morning, my dad had to even argue with her just to get up out of bed and get my sister ready for school. She'd wake up with an attitude and start stressing out my dad until he gets to the point where he beats her up and puts her out the house. She'd just go somewhere up in skyway to some white man's house and have sex with him for crack and shelter.

But my dad was not the bad guy. Kenyata had five kids' one sixteen, nine, and three. She also had two twins that are not my dads. But my dad took care of the three year old even though when

he had put her out and she left for five years, she came back pregnant with another man's baby. Then my dad and I were taking care of the baby and mostly me when they'd go to the casino at 12:00 o clock at night. The baby would wake up looking for his mom. One year went by and then the baby's dad wanted to be a dad and take care of the baby so he started trying to call Child Protective Services (C.P.S) so he can start the

58

process on getting his son. C.P.S. took Kenyata to court to get the baby full custody and Kenyata [handwritten: greatt dad] didn't go to court. Even though my dad tried waking her up, she got up with an attitude and started walking around with a stinky face. When my dad asked if she was going to court, she got mad and said get off me and stuff like that. My dad said to her, "B*TCH…if you don't get up off your raggedy a*s and go to court for your son B*TCH…" and then she left the house and didn't come back for three days. [handwritten: months]

Almost every day my dad would tell her she had the easiest life because she had five kids and doesn't take care of none of them at all. So even though my grandmother was in her death bed, she still knew what she was talking about.

The very next afternoon while everybody was at the house my grandmother was in bad condition.

The nurses came over to talk about how my grandmother was suffering and what we were going do about it. I believe they had some Michael Jackson type medicine and the nurses gave my grandmother the first dose, and my auntie finished her off by giving

her the second dose. But before she died she asked my cousin, "who do you want to live with?" And Tinka said Auntie Joe because my auntie said all kind of bad stuff about my dad. So my Great Grandmother Chris and Tinka went to live in Auburn and then the family split up, and we lost contact when my grandmother died.

It seem that the family died when my Auntie Joe moved the O.G. of the family so far away from the family, and the family did not have all that kind of gas money to go that far out up on that hill just to go see my Great Grandmother. The family really

and said that we need to make apointments just to see my grandmother

60

grew apart, when someone said that my auntie was doing all this because she wanted the money from my grandmothers insurance. But now I don't think so.

I love my auntie and I think that she did the best she could to keep my grandmother alive, but ever since I heard that I wondered if she did do it for

the insurance? My dad was so hurt about his mom dying till he was just depressed a lot. But I think my grandmother's death brought my dad and I closer together. when I had my 12th birthday party and my dad called me in the back room and gave me a blunt, and said "light it up." Even though I thought he was playing, he was not and we so together we smoked it. That was some good weed because I fell asleep at my own party.

When my dad moved out of the house we were homeless for like six months and where sleeping over at my dad's best friend Edd's house, or sometimes in the back of my dad's Lexus car, or over at Ms. Flood's house. She was the most kind women I had known, but my dad would have to pay her son Anthony Flood so we could wash our a*s, take a bath, or even come in to warm up something to eat; so most of the time I'd just stay in the car and go to sleep. I didn't want to sleep on the couch upstairs in the house because it had bed bugs. So my little sister Kiki, dad, and me we all huddled up together in the car to go to sleep.

Also at this time Kenyata had ran off with some other *guy* and left my dad because he had no house. But my dad finally got a house and before we could move in he asked her to come back and live with us. But she said nope. She did not want

62

to come and she had a new life. That's when my dad said okay and we moved in the house even though she came back like three months after and she had the other guy's twins and said that my dad was the babies' dad. I remember him telling her, "Girl...you came back with those babies ...you nasty b*tch! I already took care of the other baby that, that fool gave you and you let him take the baby away from you."

Also when we moved in my Auntie Regina was living with us for a minute. One night she said "hey Neff, let me use your phone so I let her use it and then she had to go somewhere and she ~~she'd~~ Said She put my phone on the table. But when I checked in the morning it wasn't there. I didn't think that she took it and would never give it back. But one time during my little sister's birthday, she invited her mom and my dad's ex-girl friend came over to

Kenyata and said, "don't start no sh*t...won't be no s*it," and then it was a beef right away, even though they were cool for a minute.

I guess when everybody was outside and all the women were inside, I guess Kenyata started

whooping her butt because she ran outside to tell my dad. But Kenyata jumped on her back and took her to the ground until my dad pulled her off. That's when my ~~auntie~~ left and again Kenyata got put out. *My dads ex*

 I also recall that one time at my dad's birthday party, Kenyata and her family were supposed to cook the food and bring some liquor. But instead her and her cousin drank all the liquor, and came with no food or drink and my dad was mad about it. Like I said, the family died but I tried my hardest to keep in touch with Tinka and go up to Auburn and visit Grandma Chris. At the time however my dad and auntie where beefing. So Tinka and I would talk on Facebook or over the phone. When my grandma died I think the person it hurt most was

my cousin Tinka because, for no matter what, my grandma took care of Tinka her whole life and Tinka stayed under my grandmother's wing.

But she also raised my other cousin named Larenda, and she too was also under my grandma. If you see Tinka and Larenda together they do not at all look like sisters, because they have different dads although the same mom, which is my Auntie Cassandra.   While Tinka and her sister stay in Auburn, the family's falling more and more apart. My Great Grandma Chris misses the family and especially since she was unable to interact with any of them, including family members in Auburn.

Then a couple of months went by and she had a seizure.

Even though she had to go to the hospital, she was discharged and okay. It took all that to get the family together to go and see her. However, everybody in the family kept saying they don't want to go that far to see her because of my Auntie Joe. I don't see anything wrong with Auntie Joe, but older family members might know something that I don't. All I know is that the family wanted my Great Grandmother to come to Seattle to stay closer to the family so everybody can come and spend some time with her before she passes.

So when we came to the hospital room, it was just a weird vibe and you can tell that something was not all hunky-dory and that there were some tension in the room that was not needed. I think my Great Grandmother shouldn't have to live that far out away from the family and that we should

have all the families decide where she should live.

If you haven't noticed by now I wrote this book about my family and if you're not about family then you aren't about sh*t. You can't survive in the streets without no support.

My support was my Grandma Johnnie when my mom was all doped out and left me in the hospital, when my dad sold the food stamps and we were hungry. I always had my grandma there to support me and not only me she supported the whole family and loved you even if you did something bad to her, she still loved you like you didn't do anything to her at all.

It seemed like every time I was in need she would be right there for me and when she was sick it didn't even seem like she would deserve

something like cancer ~~but~~ but when I seen her take

her last breath it did something else to me. It

didn't feel like she was dead because she was

there for me all my young life, and this is how I

feel.

ENDING POEM

My life is hard like dried up cement

glad I was born I thank my dad for his semen

I just gaze in the stars about my grandma day dreaming

Around me is a bunch of Homies plotting and scheming

Either that or a person that's fiending

If my grandma was here now what she be thinking

And I lost my Auntie Boot from drinking

It's crazy how you can lose a person faster than blinking

And it feels like the person is still here if you're not thinking

I swear I'll give everything to have my grandma back just for one weekend

But She is in my heart the whole time what was I thinking

I swear she was just here and I need to stop day dreaming

I Need to smoke some weed right now but I need to quit fiending

I dance and rap because I ~~hear~~ ear drums

When I'm singing: hear

"I'm walking down the street all alone that's what I'm thinking

I feel like aborting the mission

Because my life sometimes is like a ship that's sinking

I'm just a young man in the body but in the mind I'm grown I rock solid like a boulder or stone

I'm

My grandma was one of a kind there's no way there can be a clone

That's why when she died I felt stuck in this world all alone

70

 I am not the average young man. If you have a conversation with me I will tell you whatever is on my mind, .I am a caring and a loving person, who does not mind sharing. I am the type of person that can be friends with anyone and I am the cool guy and I am very smart. Talented in sports and dance and I am also fit. I love to meet people and enjoy helping people.

About Young Urban Authors

Young Urban Authors has a mission to empower young adults by equipping them with the necessary tools that can lead to rewarding careers as entrepreneurs, through appreciation of the literary arts and the knowledge of available opportunities to publish their own literary work. At-risk youth are targeted for program recruitment, such as delinquents, dropouts, pregnant teens, etc; however, the program sustainable skills and careers that the publishing arts have to offer.

Here is Your Chance to Support a Great Youth Organization!

The Young Urban Authors Project is thrilled to announce that ten of the youth in our program have become published authors. These young people currently have books selling on our website as well as large online book retailers. We are so proud of their accomplishments, and want to continue providing this same opportunity to other youth in the community.

Word of our program has spread throughout the community. We now have a waiting list of young people who would like to take part in the program during the winter and spring quarter. In order to continue our mission, and make this a reality for those youth, we really need your help.

Our goal is to serve 20 youth per year. Some of these young people would not have an opportunity to achieve this on their own, nor would they have the tools to do so. The average cost for one young person in the program is $1,000.00.

Please help us reach our goal of serving 20 young people per year. Your donation is tax deductible, and we appreciate whatever you can give. Know that you are helping to empower our youth and provide a brighter future in today's world. We partnered with the Seattle Neighborhood Group in our efforts to (develop) and expand our program, providing more youth with a chance to be heard.

Checks should be made payable to, "Young Urban Authors". If you prefer to donate online, please go to our website: www.youngurbanauthors.org.

There is no better feeling then knowing you have helped a child. If you have any questions, suggestions, or comments about the Young Urban Author Project, please contact us. My contact information, as well as that of the Seattle Neighborhood Group, is provided below.

Frankie Roe,

c/o Young Urban Authors

1810 E. Yesler

Seattle, WA 98122

Seattle Youth Violence Prevention Initiative

The Seattle Youth Violence Prevention Initiative (SYVPI) tackles the issue of youth violence with an approach that incorporates evidenced-based strategies along with home-grown, youth-and community-created programs. The goals of the Initiative are to achieve a 50% reduction in juvenile court referrals for violence and a 50% reduction in suspensions and expulsions from selected middle schools due to violence-related incidents.

The Initiative funds some of these home-grown programs through Community Matching Grants. These programs supplement existing Initiative services by providing positive, healthy activities that support a safe, non-violent lifestyle. The Young Urban Authors' Project is one of the first grantees under the Community Matching Grant program. It helps to fulfill the mission of the Initiative by assisting our youth to find and share their voices through the written word.

Other YUA Titles

Found – Journey to Salvation by Tayonna Gault

Standing Alone – A collection of mini stories by Mattie Alexander

A letter to my Grandma by Kylea Spears

Flipped by Yazmine Mobley

Young Life – Hanan Soulaiman

Leading Thru Change – Standing Above the Crowd by Amina Mohammed

Long Way Down by Tajh'Nique Richardson

My Cry Out – The Story of My Tears by April Wilburn

Blasian Drive – Having the Determination to Continue by Shalena Duong

Life As It Is by Jennifer Gutierrez

The Journey of a Solid Soldier by Jimmy Phin

Hi Drama – A Collection of Short Stories by Karlina Khorn

A Walk Down Memory Lane by Monique Blockman

Wrote This Because of You by CurDesia' Hudson

16280108R00044

Made in the USA
Charleston, SC
12 December 2012